Mastering Qwen 3

A Practical Guide to Exploring and Using a Leading AI Model for Language, Reasoning, and Real-World Tasks

MILA ASHFORD

TABLE OF CONTENTS

Introduction

Artificial intelligence is no longer a concept locked within sci-fi fantasies or academic journals. It's here, real, transformative, and quietly reshaping how the world operates. Behind the headlines and industry buzz lies a revolution that's no longer dominated by Silicon Valley alone. A powerful new player has entered the arena, not as an imitator, but as an innovator. That player is **Qwen 3**, Alibaba's most advanced AI model to date.

Qwen 3 isn't just another chatbot or digital assistant. It's a monumental leap in China's AI journey—proof that cutting-edge intelligence doesn't only come from the West. It's dense and sparse, multilingual and multimodal, lightning-fast and deeply analytical. In simple terms, it's a model that doesn't just talk—it reasons, adapts, translates, codes, and thinks across complex contexts and languages. And it's open-source, accessible, and shockingly powerful.

While companies in the U.S. push boundaries with models like GPT-4 and Claude, China is no longer watching from the sidelines. With Qwen 3, Alibaba has officially declared its intent: to compete, to lead, and to redefine what it means to build large-scale intelligent systems. The AI arms race is no longer a one-sided sprint. It's a global chessboard, and Qwen 3 is a masterful opening move.

But here's the problem: AI can be overwhelming, Jargon, Parameters, Benchmarks, Architecture, It's easy to get lost in the technical noise or feel like you're on the outside looking in. That's exactly why this book exists.

This is your **user-friendly guide** to Qwen 3. Whether you're an enthusiast, a developer, a tech entrepreneur, or simply someone curious about what's next in the world of AI, this book breaks it all down—clearly, simply, and without dumbing anything down. You'll understand how Qwen 3 works, where it fits in the larger AI narrative, what makes it special, and how you can start using it yourself. No fluff, no filler—just real knowledge, plainly explained.

What you're about to read isn't just another manual. It's an exploration. A decoded roadmap of one of the most important AI developments of the decade. And by the time you finish it, you won't just know what Qwen 3 is—you'll understand what it means, what it can do, and why it may just be the model that shifts the global AI conversation for good.

Ready to discover what lies beneath the surface of Qwen 3? Let's begin.

Chapter 1

The Evolution of Qwen

From Qwen 1 to Qwen 3: The Journey of a New AI Powerhouse

The emergence of Qwen 3 didn't happen in isolation. Like all transformative technologies, it stands on the shoulders of earlier iterations—bold, experimental attempts that laid the groundwork for what has now become a landmark development in artificial intelligence. Understanding Qwen 3's evolution means tracing the steps of its predecessors and recognizing how each version pushed the boundaries of what Alibaba's AI division could achieve.

The story begins with **Qwen 1**, Alibaba's entry into the large language model (LLM) landscape. It was a foundational model, structured to prove that China's tech ecosystem could develop capabilities akin to the likes of OpenAI's GPT series or Meta's LLaMA. Built on a blend of transformer-based architecture and optimized token training strategies, Qwen 1 prioritized robust language understanding across Chinese and English. While it lacked the polished fluency and advanced reasoning of Western competitors, Qwen 1's existence marked a vital step in closing the global AI gap.

From Qwen 1 emerged **Qwen 2**, a stronger and smarter model with upgraded capabilities in logical reasoning, code generation, and multilingual support. Its release signaled a serious shift: Alibaba wasn't simply replicating ideas—it was refining them. Qwen 2 featured better training alignment with human preferences, as well as improved memory handling and contextual awareness. This allowed it to generate more accurate and contextually relevant responses, not just mimicry. Early adopters in academic, enterprise, and open-source circles started to take notice.

Yet, even with Qwen 2's improvements, the model hadn't fully cracked the ceiling. It still lagged behind in areas like multimodal processing, dynamic tool use, and parameter efficiency compared to state-of-the-art Western models. That's where **Qwen 3** came in—not as an upgrade, but as a transformation. The leap from Qwen 2 to Qwen 3 wasn't linear; it was exponential. The architecture was redesigned, the training data diversified, and the ambition scaled up dramatically.

Qwen 3 was introduced not just as a model, but as a **family** of models, ranging from lightweight mobile-compatible versions like Qwen1.5-0.5B to heavyweights such as Qwen1.5-72B. This modular approach allowed developers to tailor performance to their needs—balancing speed, memory, and precision. What's more, these models could understand and generate content in multiple languages, handle images as well as text, write code, and reason with greater depth than any previous Qwen version.

The release of Qwen 3 signaled that Alibaba wasn't content with catching up—it was ready to compete at the highest level. It came with transparent open-source licensing, pre-trained and instruction-tuned versions, and a focus on accessibility for both researchers and businesses. This shift wasn't just technical; it was philosophical. Alibaba was opening its AI ecosystem to the world, and Qwen 3 was its flagship.

From its earliest form to the powerhouse it has become, the Qwen series represents a remarkable journey of innovation. Each version built strategically on the last, incorporating global trends while infusing unique local priorities—such as strong Chinese language performance and integration with Alibaba's vast digital ecosystem. Now, with Qwen 3, the model doesn't just reflect the past—it defines the future of Alibaba's AI vision.

What Sets Qwen 3 Apart from Its Predecessors

Qwen 3 isn't just another notch in a version history—it's a blueprint for what next-generation AI should look like. At its core, Qwen 3 introduces sweeping enhancements in scale, performance, architecture, training methodology, and openness. But the real distinction lies in how these improvements translate into real-world capabilities.

1. A Model Family, Not Just a Single Release

One of the most innovative features of Qwen 3 is its structure as a **model family**. Instead of a one-size-fits-all release, Alibaba designed Qwen 3 in multiple sizes: 0.5B, 1.8B, 4B, 7B, 14B, and 72B parameters. This means developers, researchers, and enterprises can select a version that best suits their computational environment—whether it's a smartphone app, a research tool, or a commercial backend AI system.

This scale-aware design makes Qwen 3 highly adaptable, bringing advanced capabilities to lightweight environments without sacrificing speed or reliability. It's a practical evolution in an industry that often forces users to choose between power and usability.

2. Superior Training and Instruction Tuning

Qwen 3 has been instruction-tuned to understand complex queries and deliver outputs that closely match human expectations. Unlike its predecessors, it doesn't just generate information—it **follows intent**. The result is higher response accuracy, less hallucination, and a much more natural conversation flow. Its instruction-following ability mirrors top-tier models like GPT-4 and Claude, placing it firmly in the same competitive arena.

3. True Multilingual Fluency

Where previous Qwen versions emphasized Chinese and English, Qwen 3 elevates multilingual capability to a new level. It handles **code-switching**, **translation**, and

multilingual prompts with ease, making it ideal for global deployment. Whether you're prompting in French, Japanese, or Hindi, Qwen 3 can understand and respond with contextual relevance.

4.   Multimodal   Understanding

Qwen-VL (Vision Language) variants in the Qwen 3 family can analyze **both text and images**. This makes them perfect for use cases in e-commerce, digital content moderation, medical imaging, and intelligent document processing. The model can caption, classify, extract information from images, and even reason about visual data in ways that are useful to both consumers and professionals.

5.   Open-Source   Commitment

Perhaps one of the most strategic

differentiators is Alibaba's decision to **open-source** the Qwen 3 models under an **Apache 2.0 license**. This is a bold move in a world where AI giants often gatekeep access. By opening the architecture and weights, Alibaba invites global collaboration, transparency, and innovation. This instantly sets Qwen 3 apart from commercial closed models while also boosting trust and adoption in research communities.

6. Dense and Mixture-of-Experts Architectures

Qwen 3 blends **dense transformer models** with **Mixture-of-Experts (MoE)** strategies to optimize both performance and training efficiency. The MoE design allows different parts of the model to specialize in different tasks, boosting overall capability without ballooning compute requirements. This allows Qwen 3 to scale intelligently, making better use of hardware and data resources.

7. Compatibility with Tool Use and Plugins

In keeping with trends set by GPT-4 and Claude 3, Qwen 3 supports **tool calling**, meaning it can interface with plugins, APIs, and external databases. This opens doors to real-world integration in fintech, logistics, and enterprise-level automation. Qwen 3 can become a thinking assistant, not just a talking one.

Taken together, these advancements put Qwen 3 in the league of the most advanced LLMs available today. It's not just better than its predecessors—it's on a whole new plane.

How Alibaba Positioned Itself as a Global AI Contender

For years, the narrative around AI leadership was dominated by U.S. companies—OpenAI, Google DeepMind, Meta, Anthropic. China's AI efforts, while significant, often appeared siloed or domestically focused. But Alibaba's strategic approach to Qwen 3 has changed the game. This isn't a quiet local experiment; it's a loud declaration that China is ready to lead in AI on a global scale.

1. Global-Ready Open Models By releasing Qwen 3 under open licenses and ensuring documentation is accessible in English and Chinese, Alibaba sends a clear message: this is a model for the world. Unlike proprietary competitors, Qwen 3 welcomes global developers, researchers, and enterprises to build, adapt, and scale it.

2.   Infrastructure   Integration

Alibaba doesn't operate in a vacuum. It owns massive cloud infrastructure through Alibaba Cloud, operates a vast e-commerce ecosystem, and manages logistics, fintech, and media services—all of which benefit from AI optimization. Qwen 3 is already being integrated across this network, giving Alibaba a uniquely holistic AI footprint that few companies in the West can match.

3. Strategic Model Design for Scale

Qwen 3 was designed not only to compete with current models but to **scale efficiently over time**. Its model family structure allows for deployment on everything from edge devices to supercomputers, positioning Alibaba to serve both emerging markets and high-tech economies.

4. Collaboration over Competition
By open-sourcing Qwen 3, Alibaba chose **collaboration as a form of power**. It aligns with China's broader strategy of AI diplomacy—using shared models, cross-border academic alliances, and global access to build influence. This is a stark contrast to the guarded, closed-loop development seen in many U.S. labs.

5. Real-World Applications at Scale
Alibaba has already embedded Qwen 3 into its e-commerce platforms, intelligent customer service bots, warehouse automation systems, and content moderation workflows. This gives the model

a **real-world testing ground** with billions of interactions, allowing for rapid iteration and grounded optimization—something many research labs can only simulate.

6. National Support and Long-Term Vision

Alibaba's AI endeavors are supported by China's broader **national innovation agenda**. With government backing, talent pipeline investments, and access to strategic compute resources, Qwen 3 benefits from a long-term runway that goes beyond quarterly results. It is not just a corporate experiment—it's part of a national vision.

In short, Alibaba has transformed from a regional tech titan to a serious global AI contender. Through technical sophistication, strategic openness, and real-world integration, Qwen 3 isn't just a model—it's a message. China is not only catching up in AI—it's setting the pace.

Chapter 2

Inside Qwen 3's Architecture

The architecture of a large language model like Qwen 3 is fundamental to its performance, scalability, and adaptability. With a variety of design choices, including a combination of dense and sparse (Mixture-of-Experts, or MoE) systems, Qwen 3 introduces an innovative hybrid approach to AI modeling.

The Hybrid Model: What It Means to Combine Dense and Sparse (MoE) Systems

Qwen 3 represents a significant leap in model architecture through its **hybrid approach** to artificial intelligence. In simple terms, a hybrid model blends the benefits of two distinct kinds of systems: **dense models** and **sparse models** (the latter implemented via **Mixture-of-Experts, MoE**). Each of these approaches has its advantages and limitations, and Qwen 3 maximizes the strengths of both.

Dense Models

Traditionally, large language models (LLMs) like GPT-3, GPT-4, and many others follow the **dense model** approach. A dense model utilizes a set number of parameters that are active across all inputs, processing every part of the model to handle a given task. This results in a system where each parameter is engaged regardless of the input, ensuring uniform attention to all data.

The primary benefit of a dense model is its simplicity and consistency. Every parameter is always available for any input, which can improve performance when all the parameters are needed to process complex, multi-faceted tasks. However, this architecture can become computationally expensive as the number of parameters increases, leading to inefficiencies when the task at hand doesn't require the full capacity of the model.

Sparse Models and the Rise of MoE

To overcome the limitations of dense models, Qwen 3 introduces **sparse models** through a system called **Mixture-of-Experts (MoE)**. MoE is a form of architecture where only a subset of the total model parameters is activated for each specific input. In simpler terms, instead of using all of the model's parameters for every task, MoE dynamically selects a subset of parameters, or **"experts,"** to handle the input data.

This selective activation of parameters allows for greater efficiency, as it reduces the computational load while still retaining the model's ability to process complex tasks. The **Mixture-of-Experts** approach is particularly well-suited for tasks that require deep specialization—by training different experts for different tasks, Qwen 3 ensures that the model's efficiency improves without sacrificing performance.

Advantages of MoE

- **Efficiency**: MoE models activate fewer parameters per task, significantly reducing computational costs.

- **Specialization**: Experts can specialize in specific aspects of language, such as natural language understanding, code generation, or text summarization.

- **Scalability**: MoE models allow for scaling to extremely large models without the corresponding increase in computational requirements.

However, the MoE system also introduces complexity in model training and management. By choosing different experts for each input, Qwen 3 must dynamically determine which experts are needed for each task, a process that involves sophisticated coordination and resource management.

Hybrid Approach in Qwen 3

Qwen 3's architecture utilizes the best of both dense and sparse models. The model dynamically switches between the dense and MoE layers depending on the nature of the task and the input data. This hybrid model maximizes the efficiency of MoE for large, complex tasks while leveraging the simplicity and robustness of dense models when uniform processing is required.

Model Variants and Their Parameter Sizes: 0.6B to 235B Explained

One of the most striking features of Qwen 3's architecture is its **variability** in model sizes. The Qwen 3 family consists of models ranging from smaller, more lightweight versions with as few as **0.6 billion parameters** to large-scale models with a staggering **235 billion parameters**. These different variants cater to different use cases, from edge devices and mobile applications to enterprise-level systems and research projects.

Smaller Models (0.6B – 4B Parameters)

The smaller Qwen 3 models, such as the **0.6B** and **1B** versions, are optimized for efficiency, making them ideal for **edge devices** and **mobile applications**. These versions prioritize quick responses and reduced computational demands while still maintaining core functionalities like natural language understanding and generation. These models are designed to run efficiently on devices with limited resources—such as smartphones, tablets, and even embedded systems—without the need for powerful cloud infrastructure.

Use Cases for Smaller Models:

- **Mobile apps**: Allowing real-time AI-powered interactions and personalization on smartphones.

- **Edge computing**: Enabling AI processing on devices like drones, wearables, and IoT systems.

- **Personal assistants**: Providing seamless, localized, and efficient AI responses for personal or enterprise use.

The smaller models represent the **scalable AI approach**, enabling Qwen 3's capabilities to be deployed across a vast range of applications, all while maintaining a small resource footprint.

Mid-Range Models (7B – 30B Parameters)

The mid-range models, such as those with **7B** or **14B** parameters, strike a balance between computational efficiency and performance. These versions are ideal for **enterprise applications** and **large-scale systems** that require robust performance but don't have the same resource constraints as smaller devices.

Use Cases for Mid-Range Models:

- **Business intelligence**: Automating workflows and generating insights from large data sets.

- **Customer service bots**: Providing intelligent, context-aware assistance in e-commerce and enterprise environments.

- **Content generation**: Enhancing creative workflows in industries like advertising, publishing, and entertainment.

These models are designed to handle more complex tasks that require significant language understanding, reasoning, and problem-solving abilities, while still providing faster response times and lower resource consumption than their larger counterparts.

Large Models (72B – 235B Parameters)

The **largest models** in the Qwen 3 family—those with **72B** and up to **235B parameters**—are designed for **high-performance, computationally intensive tasks**. These versions incorporate the full power of the **Mixture-of-Experts (MoE)** architecture, ensuring they can handle complex, multi-step reasoning, text generation, and multimodal tasks.

Use Cases for Large Models:

- **Scientific research**: Assisting in data analysis, hypothesis generation, and computational modeling in areas like biology, physics, and chemistry.

- **Advanced content creation**: Generating high-quality, nuanced content for industries like filmmaking, gaming, and high-level academia.

- **Large-scale automation**: Powering enterprise-level AI systems capable of handling millions of interactions per second with dynamic decision-making.

The 235B version represents the **pinnacle of Qwen 3's capability**, suitable for industries where performance and precision are paramount, and the cost of running the system is justified by the task complexity.

The Purpose Behind Dense vs. Sparse Versions

Qwen 3's hybrid architecture, combining both dense and sparse (MoE) models, is not just a technical innovation—it has a **purpose** rooted in **practical AI deployment** across various domains. To understand why this distinction between dense and sparse versions matters, let's dive deeper into the **strategic choices** behind the two types of models.

Dense Models: Universal Reliability

Dense models are optimized for scenarios where **uniform processing** is needed for all inputs. These models are reliable because they use all available parameters to process data, ensuring that they can handle a wide range of tasks with consistent quality. While dense models can be computationally expensive, their **predictable behavior** makes them ideal for critical applications that demand **high accuracy** and **robustness**.

Use Cases for Dense Models:

- **Core AI functions**: Tasks that require universal intelligence, such as question answering, sentiment analysis, and language translation.

- **High-complexity tasks**: Activities that involve deep reasoning or require processing large sets of variables simultaneously.

Dense models in Qwen 3 are typically used in **situations where performance consistency and reliability** are paramount—especially in applications that require precision and stability across a broad range of data types.

Sparse Models (MoE): Specialized Efficiency

In contrast, sparse models (MoE) are highly **efficient** because they only activate a subset of the model's parameters, focusing on the most relevant parts of the architecture for a given task. This makes MoE models incredibly **cost-effective**, allowing them to scale to much larger sizes without overwhelming available computational resources.

However, sparse models come with their own set of advantages that make them **ideal for highly specialized applications** where specific knowledge is required. The **flexibility** of MoE allows Qwen 3 to optimize for tasks that benefit from **specialized expertise**, such as visual data analysis, advanced medical research, and tailored customer service.

Use Cases for Sparse Models (MoE):

- **Task-specific applications**: Analyzing visual data, recommending products, or processing specific industries' technical language.

- **Large-scale systems**: Enabling cost-effective, specialized intelligence at scale, such as personal assistants or advanced chatbots.

- **Real-time data processing**: Performing actions like speech recognition or monitoring vast amounts of data in real time.

By combining dense and sparse models, Qwen 3 achieves a balanced architecture that **optimizes for both performance and efficiency**, scaling easily across devices and industries.

How MoE (Mixture-of-Experts) Works in Practice

The Mixture-of-Experts (MoE) system is one of the most revolutionary aspects of Qwen 3's architecture. It fundamentally changes how large language models operate by dynamically activating only a subset of the model's total parameters for each task. In practice, this means that while Qwen 3 might have hundreds of billions of parameters in total, only a small fraction are used at any given time. This targeted selection allows the model to optimize performance without the need to engage every parameter for each individual input.

How MoE Operates

At the core of the MoE system is the concept of "experts." These experts are specialized sub-networks within the larger model, each trained to handle specific types of tasks or data. During model operation, when an input is presented to Qwen 3, the model activates a particular set of experts that are best suited to process that input. This is known as **routing**. The routing mechanism uses an algorithm to select which experts should be activated based on the input data's characteristics. This ensures that only the most relevant parts of the model are used, improving efficiency without sacrificing the depth of understanding.

For example, when Qwen 3 is tasked with processing a piece of legal text, the routing mechanism might activate experts that have specialized in legal terminology, grammar, and contextual knowledge. On the other hand, when asked to generate creative writing, it may activate a different set of experts that specialize in narrative techniques, tone generation, and style.

This dynamic routing is a defining feature of MoE, as it allows the model to **scale intelligently**. Instead of requiring every expert to be involved in every task, MoE ensures that computational resources are only used when they're needed.

Benefits of MoE in Practice

The implementation of MoE brings several benefits to Qwen 3, especially as the model scales to larger sizes.

1. Scalability

MoE allows Qwen 3 to scale to immense sizes without incurring the same computational costs as traditional dense models. By activating only a fraction of the model's parameters at any given time, Qwen 3 can handle much larger architectures (with up to 235 billion parameters) without the need for proportionally more computing resources. This allows developers and enterprises to deploy Qwen 3 for demanding tasks without overwhelming their infrastructure.

2. Specialization

Another significant advantage of MoE is its ability to specialize. As mentioned earlier, different experts within the MoE system are trained on different tasks or types of data. This means that Qwen 3 can **deeply specialize** in areas like **legal analysis,** medical diagnostics, creative content generation, and more. It can become an expert in multiple domains while still maintaining high levels of performance and efficiency in each one. This specialization is particularly useful for industries that require a deep understanding of niche subjects but also need AI systems to scale.

3. Cost Efficiency

By not activating the entire model for every single input, MoE ensures that Qwen 3 is highly cost-effective in terms of computational requirements. This efficiency is particularly important in commercial and enterprise environments, where AI models need to process vast amounts of data but must remain affordable and scalable. The cost savings from using MoE instead of a fully dense model are substantial, especially when applied at the large scale that Qwen 3 supports.

4. Flexibility

MoE provides an unparalleled level of **flexibility** in how Qwen 3 can be utilized. Since different experts specialize in different domains, the model can be tuned to focus on specific areas of interest or expertise. Whether it's understanding finance, generating poetry, or solving complex scientific problems, Qwen 3 can adapt its expert selection to fit the task at hand, making it an incredibly versatile tool for diverse industries.

Challenges of MoE and How Qwen 3 Addresses Them

While MoE brings many advantages, it is not without its challenges. For example, **dynamic routing**—the process of selecting which experts to activate—requires careful management to ensure that the system remains efficient. Without proper routing algorithms, MoE can become inefficient and fail to deliver the expected performance improvements.

Qwen 3 addresses these challenges by using a sophisticated routing mechanism that ensures the right experts are selected for the right tasks. This mechanism is designed to be both **adaptive** and **efficient**, continuously learning from its previous decisions to improve the selection of experts.

Additionally, MoE systems can sometimes experience **sparse utilization**—meaning that some experts may rarely be activated, leading to underutilization of resources. To combat this, Qwen 3 includes optimization strategies that ensure all experts are sufficiently engaged, preventing waste and ensuring that the model remains balanced.

The Role of MoE in Qwen 3's Performance

MoE's impact on Qwen 3's performance cannot be understated. By utilizing expert specialization and dynamically selecting which parts of the model are active at any given time, Qwen 3 achieves **impressive speed and scalability**. These attributes make Qwen 3 one of the most **efficient and high-performance language models** available today. The model can handle complex tasks, such as natural language understanding, text generation, and multimodal data processing, while remaining cost-effective and adaptable.

Furthermore, the ability to scale with MoE means that Qwen 3 can continuously evolve as new experts are added to the system. As new industries or tasks emerge, Qwen 3 can incorporate **new specialists** into the model, ensuring that it remains at the cutting edge of AI development.

Qwen 3's architecture represents a breakthrough in AI model design, combining the best of both dense and sparse models through its hybrid approach. By leveraging **Mixture-of-Experts (MoE)** technology, Qwen 3 offers **unparalleled scalability**, **efficiency**, and **specialization**. The model's diverse variants—ranging from small, efficient models for edge devices to massive, high-performance systems for enterprise use—demonstrate its adaptability across a broad range of applications.

The introduction of MoE brings about **flexibility**, ensuring that Qwen 3 can specialize in a vast array of domains while maintaining efficiency in the process. As a result, Qwen 3 is not only one of the most capable AI systems in existence, but also one of the most **resource-efficient** and **future-proof** models on the market.

Chapter 3

What Powers Qwen 3

In the rapidly advancing world of artificial intelligence, each new model builds on the previous generation's capabilities. With the launch of Qwen 3, Alibaba has truly raised the bar for what AI systems can achieve. Powering Qwen 3 are several key features that contribute to its unmatched performance, versatility, and scalability.

Training Scale: 36 Trillion Tokens and Why That's a Big Deal

One of the key features that sets Qwen 3 apart from its predecessors is its extraordinary training scale. The model has been trained on **36 trillion tokens**—a staggering amount of data that plays a significant role in the model's ability to generate highly accurate, context-aware, and nuanced responses.

What Are Tokens and Why Do They Matter?

Before diving into the significance of Qwen 3's training scale, it's important to understand what tokens are and why they matter in AI model training. In simple terms, **tokens** represent chunks of text that the AI model processes. A token can be a word, part of a word, or even punctuation marks. For instance, the sentence "Qwen 3 is a game changer" could be broken down into several tokens like "Qwen", "3", "is", "a", "game", "changer."

The **size of the training data**—measured in tokens—determines how well the AI model can understand and generate natural language. The larger the dataset, the more diverse the information the model can learn from. In the case of Qwen 3, the sheer scale of 36 trillion tokens gives it an unprecedented **depth of understanding** and the ability to make highly accurate predictions based on a wide range of inputs.

The Importance of 36 Trillion Tokens

Qwen 3's training on **36 trillion tokens** is a significant achievement in the field of AI. To put this into perspective, earlier models like GPT-3 were trained on only around **570**

billion tokens. The scale of Qwen 3's training data gives it several advantages over smaller models, including:

1. **Comprehensive Knowledge Base**: With a training set of 36 trillion tokens, Qwen 3 has access to an incredibly vast range of information, including diverse linguistic patterns, subject matter expertise, cultural contexts, and historical data. This extensive dataset allows the model to be more versatile and provide more accurate responses across different domains.

2. **Increased Generalization Capabilities**: A larger dataset enables Qwen 3 to generalize better

across various topics. The model is able to understand subtleties in language and produce responses that are not only contextually accurate but also highly nuanced and sophisticated. It can handle a wider range of inquiries, from technical explanations to creative writing, and generate responses that feel more human-like.

3. **Minimizing Bias and Errors**: With a diverse training dataset, Qwen 3 has a better chance of minimizing biases that may be present in smaller datasets. A model trained on a large variety of sources is more likely to represent a balanced view, offering a better understanding of different

perspectives, opinions, and topics.

4. **Improved Performance Across Tasks**: The massive scale of training data enables Qwen 3 to excel in multiple domains, from answering factual questions to engaging in complex reasoning tasks. Whether it's generating text, solving problems, or understanding complex technical jargon, Qwen 3 can handle tasks with incredible accuracy.

The Computational Challenges of Training at Such Scale

Training a model on such a large scale requires immense computational power and resources. Qwen 3's training involved state-of-the-art hardware and distributed computing systems, ensuring that the model could process and learn from trillions of tokens efficiently. This computational prowess allows Qwen 3 to handle tasks that would have been impossible for smaller models.

Support for 119 Languages and Dialects: Breaking Linguistic Barriers

Language is a powerful tool for communication, but with over 7,000 languages spoken worldwide, it can also be a barrier. One of the standout features of Qwen 3 is its ability to **understand and generate text in 119 different languages and dialects**, making it an incredibly versatile AI model that can be used across the globe.

Why Multilingual Support is Important

In today's interconnected world, businesses and organizations require tools that can cross language barriers and communicate effectively with global audiences. With Qwen 3 supporting **119 languages**, it has the ability to reach a broad, diverse user base and serve as an essential tool for international business, translation, customer service, and more.

Diverse Linguistic Features in Qwen 3

Qwen 3 doesn't just support multiple languages—it's designed to handle a wide range of **dialects** and regional variations within those languages. This means that Qwen 3 can provide localized responses tailored to the user's cultural and linguistic context. Whether you're speaking Mandarin with a southern Chinese dialect, or you need a translation from Spanish to a specific Argentinian variant, Qwen 3 has the capabilities to understand and process these nuances.

Applications of Multilingual Capabilities

The multilingual support in Qwen 3 opens up several possibilities for businesses, developers, and individuals:

1. **Global Customer Support**:
   Businesses that operate internationally can use Qwen 3 to

provide multilingual customer service, ensuring that customers in different countries receive support in their native languages.

2. **Translation Services**: Qwen 3 can act as a powerful translation tool, capable of translating text or speech from one language to another while maintaining the integrity of the original meaning.

3. **Cultural Sensitivity**: By understanding not just the language but also the cultural context behind it, Qwen 3 can provide responses that are culturally sensitive and appropriate for different regions.

4. **Education and Content Creation**: Educational platforms and content creators can leverage Qwen 3 to create learning materials in multiple languages, broadening access to high-quality content for global audiences.

Overcoming Linguistic Challenges

Multilingual AI models face significant challenges, such as differences in grammar, syntax, and cultural references. However, Qwen 3's architecture is designed to tackle these complexities. By training on large, diverse multilingual datasets, the model is capable of handling languages with different structures (like the agglutinative nature of Turkish or the tonal characteristics of

Mandarin) while providing accurate and contextually correct responses.

The 128,000-Token Context Window: Long-Form Thinking in AI

Another remarkable feature of Qwen 3 is its **128,000-token context window**, a substantial leap from the token limits seen in earlier models. To understand the significance of this, let's first explore what a **context window** is and how it impacts the model's ability to perform tasks.

What Is a Context Window?

In AI language models, the context window refers to the amount of text the model can consider when generating a response. When

Qwen 3 is given an input, it breaks the text into tokens and processes them within a specific window of tokens. The larger the context window, the more information the model can analyze at once, allowing it to make better-informed predictions.

For example, with a smaller context window (like 4,000 or 8,000 tokens), the model may only be able to consider a few paragraphs of text at a time. However, Qwen 3's ability to handle 128,000 tokens allows it to process entire documents, long conversations, or multi-chapter texts all at once.

Why a Larger Context Window Matters

1. **Long-Form Content Understanding:** A larger context window means that

Qwen 3 can handle long-form content, such as essays, books, research papers, and multi-part conversations, without losing coherence. The model can remember and relate information across larger spans of text, leading to more **relevant, contextually-aware responses**.

2. **Better Long-Term Reasoning**: When analyzing complex topics, Qwen 3 can consider more of the relevant background information, leading to deeper insights and more accurate predictions. For instance, when answering a question about a historical event that spans several paragraphs or pages, the model can pull from all of that information rather

than just the most recent section.

3. **Multi-Turn Conversations**: In conversational settings, a larger context window allows the model to track longer exchanges and maintain **coherent dialogue** over multiple turns. It can refer back to earlier parts of the conversation to ensure continuity, making interactions more **natural** and **fluid**.

4. **Improved Memory for Detailed Tasks**: Whether it's solving a complex mathematical problem, analyzing legal documents, or generating a piece of creative writing, Qwen 3's expanded context window helps ensure that the model doesn't forget important details

as it processes a long sequence of input.

Impact on User Experience

The 128,000-token context window significantly improves the overall user experience, particularly in situations where users need **comprehensive answers**, **thorough analysis**, or **detailed, multi-step problem solving**. This expanded window allows Qwen 3 to function as a **long-form thinking machine**, one that can handle tasks that require deep understanding and continuity over extended periods.

How the Tokenizer Enables Hybrid Reasoning

The **tokenizer** plays a critical role in enabling Qwen 3's hybrid reasoning capabilities. At a basic level, the tokenizer breaks down input text into tokens that the AI model can process. However, its functionality extends far beyond this basic task, helping to facilitate **complex reasoning** and **multimodal thinking** within the model.

Hybrid Reasoning in Qwen 3

Hybrid reasoning refers to the model's ability to combine different types of cognitive approaches—such as **deductive reasoning**, **inductive reasoning**, and **abductive reasoning**—to solve complex tasks. The tokenizer helps the model integrate **logical** and **creative** thinking, allowing it to switch between different reasoning modes depending on the task at hand.

For example, when generating creative writing, Qwen 3 might use inductive reasoning to draw from a variety of influences and craft a narrative. On the other hand, when answering a factual question, it may use deductive reasoning to narrow down the possibilities and arrive at the most likely answer.

Enabling Multimodal Reasoning

Additionally, the tokenizer in Qwen 3 supports **multimodal reasoning**, enabling the model to process and combine different forms of input—text, images, and other media. This allows Qwen 3 to generate responses that integrate information from various sources, leading to a **richer, more nuanced** understanding of complex topics.

Qwen 3's advanced features—its immense training scale, multilingual capabilities, large context window, and tokenizer-driven hybrid reasoning—empower the model to solve problems and provide insights that were previously out of reach for traditional AI systems. By handling vast amounts of data and understanding multiple languages, Qwen 3 is well-equipped to break down barriers, improve efficiency, and pave the way for more intelligent, context-aware AI applications across the globe.

In the next chapter, we will explore how developers and businesses can leverage these powerful features to integrate Qwen 3 into real-world applications. From **customized**

chatbots to **advanced research tools**, Qwen 3 offers a wide range of possibilities for innovation. Stay tuned as we dive deeper into practical use cases for this groundbreaking model.

Chapter 4

Exploring the Capabilities of Qwen 3

Alibaba's Qwen 3 represents a significant advancement in the field of artificial intelligence, offering a suite of capabilities that extend beyond traditional language models. With its hybrid architecture, extensive multilingual support, robust code generation, and multimodal functionalities, Qwen 3 is poised to redefine the boundaries of AI applications.

Natural Language Understanding and Generation

At the core of Qwen 3 lies its exceptional natural language understanding (NLU) and generation (NLG) capabilities. Trained on a vast corpus of 36 trillion tokens, Qwen 3 demonstrates a profound grasp of linguistic nuances, enabling it to comprehend and generate human-like text across diverse contexts.

The model's architecture allows it to process and generate text with remarkable coherence and relevance. Whether summarizing complex documents, engaging in conversational dialogues, or crafting creative narratives, Qwen 3 maintains contextual integrity and fluency. Its ability to handle long-form content is further enhanced by a 128,000-token context window, allowing it to consider extensive textual inputs without losing track of the overarching theme or specific details.

Moreover, Qwen 3's NLU and NLG capabilities are not confined to English. The model's training data encompasses a diverse range of languages and dialects, ensuring its applicability in a global context. This multilingual proficiency is instrumental in tasks such as translation, cross-cultural communication, and content localization.

Multilingual Fluency and Real-World Use Cases

Qwen 3's support for 119 languages and dialects positions it as a truly global AI model. This extensive linguistic coverage enables seamless communication across diverse linguistic communities, breaking down language barriers and fostering inclusivity.

In practical applications, Qwen 3's multilingual capabilities are transformative. For instance, businesses can deploy Qwen 3-powered chatbots to provide customer support in multiple languages, enhancing user experience and expanding market reach. Educational platforms can utilize the model to offer multilingual content, catering to a broader audience and promoting equitable access to information.

Furthermore, Qwen 3's proficiency in various languages facilitates accurate and context-aware translations. Unlike traditional translation tools that may struggle with idiomatic expressions or cultural nuances, Qwen 3's deep learning framework allows it to capture the subtleties of language, ensuring more natural and meaningful translations.Gradient Flow

Code Generation and Reasoning Logic

Beyond natural language processing, Qwen 3 exhibits robust capabilities in code generation and logical reasoning. The model's architecture supports a "thinking mode," enabling it to tackle complex tasks that require analytical and deductive reasoning. This mode is particularly effective in generating code snippets, solving mathematical problems, and performing data analysis.

Qwen 3's code generation proficiency is evident in its ability to understand programming languages and generate syntactically correct and functional code. Developers can leverage this feature to automate coding tasks, debug existing codebases, or even learn new programming concepts through interactive sessions with the model.

The model's reasoning logic extends to various domains, including scientific research, finance, and engineering. By processing complex datasets and drawing logical inferences, Qwen 3 can assist in hypothesis testing, risk assessment, and strategic planning. Its capacity to handle intricate reasoning tasks makes it a valuable tool for professionals seeking data-driven insights.

Multimodal Abilities: Beyond Text

Qwen 3's capabilities transcend text-based processing, encompassing multimodal functionalities that integrate visual and auditory data. This multimodal approach enables the model to interpret and generate content across different media types, enhancing its versatility and applicability.

In the realm of image processing, Qwen 3 can analyze visual inputs to extract meaningful information, describe scenes, or generate relevant textual content. This feature is particularly beneficial in fields like digital marketing, where generating captions or product descriptions based on images can streamline content creation processes.

The model's auditory capabilities allow it to process and generate speech, facilitating applications such as voice assistants, transcription services, and language learning tools. By understanding and producing spoken language, Qwen 3 can engage users in more natural and interactive ways.Qwen

Moreover, Qwen 3's multimodal functionalities support the development of applications that require the integration of text, images, and audio. For example, educational platforms can create immersive learning experiences by combining textual explanations with visual aids and auditory feedback, catering to diverse learning styles and enhancing comprehension.

Qwen 3 represents a significant leap forward in AI capabilities, offering a comprehensive suite of features that address a wide array of applications. Its advanced natural language processing, multilingual fluency, code generation proficiency, and multimodal functionalities position it as a versatile and powerful tool across various industries. As AI continues to evolve, models like Qwen 3 will play a pivotal role in shaping the future of human-computer interaction, driving innovation, and fostering global connectivity.

Chapter 5

Using Qwen 3—Where and How

Alibaba's Qwen 3 stands as a testament to the evolution of open-source AI, offering developers, researchers, and enterprises a versatile tool for various applications.

Accessing Qwen 3

Platforms and Resources

Qwen 3 is accessible through multiple platforms, ensuring that users can choose the environment that best suits their needs.

GitHub

Alibaba maintains the Qwen 3 repositories on GitHub, providing access to model weights, configuration files, and documentation. This platform is ideal for developers seeking to delve into the model's architecture or contribute to its development.

Hugging Face

Hugging Face hosts various Qwen 3 models, including the Qwen3-30B-A3B and its base versions. Users can utilize these models directly through the Hugging Face Transformers library or deploy them using tools like vLLM and SGLang. Medium+4Qwen+4DigitalOcean+4Hugging Face+3LinkedIn+3Qwen+3

ModelScope

ModelScope offers a curated collection of Qwen 3 models, catering to users interested in specific applications or configurations. This platform provides pre-trained models optimized for various tasks, facilitating easier integration into projects.

Chat.Qwen.ai

For users seeking an interactive experience, Chat.Qwen.ai provides a web-based interface to engage with Qwen 3. This platform showcases the model's capabilities in real-time, allowing users to explore its potential without any setup.

Setting Up and Deploying Qwen 3 Models

Deploying Qwen 3 can be tailored to various environments, from local machines to cloud infrastructures.

Local Deployment

For developers aiming to run Qwen 3 locally, tools like Ollama and vLLM offer streamlined solutions.DigitalOcean+5Hugging Face+5Qwen+5

- **Ollama**: A user-friendly tool that simplifies the process of running large language models locally. It's compatible with macOS, Linux, and

Windows. Hugging Face

- **vLLM**: An efficient inference engine optimized for large language models, ensuring high throughput and low latency.

These tools facilitate the deployment of Qwen 3 on personal devices, enabling developers to experiment and build applications without relying on external servers.

Cloud Deployment

For scalable and production-ready deployments, cloud platforms offer robust solutions.

- **NodeShift Cloud**: Provides GPU-powered virtual machines tailored for AI workloads. Users can select GPU models, configure resources, and deploy Qwen 3 seamlessly. DigitalOcean+2DEV Community+2LinkedIn+2

- **Predibase**: Offers private cloud deployments of Qwen 3 on platforms like AWS, GCP, or Azure, ensuring enterprise-grade privacy and performance. predibase.com

These platforms cater to businesses and researchers requiring robust infrastructure and scalability.

Understanding the Apache 2.0 License: Embracing Open-Source

Qwen 3 is released under the Apache License 2.0, a permissive open-source license that grants users significant freedoms.FOSSA

Key Features of Apache 2.0

- **Commercial Use**: Users can freely use, modify, and distribute the software, even in proprietary applications.

- **Modification and Distribution**: The license allows for modifications and the distribution of derivative works, provided that proper attribution is maintained.Wikipedia

- **Patent Grant**: Contributors provide an express grant of patent rights, offering legal protection to users.

- **No Warranty**: The software is provided "as-is," without warranties or conditions of any kind.tldrlegal.com

This licensing model encourages widespread adoption and integration, reducing legal complexities and fostering innovation.FOSSA+2WIRED+2Wikipedia+2

Integration Opportunities for Developers and Businesses

Qwen 3's versatility opens doors for various integration scenarios across industries.

Developers

For individual developers and small teams, Qwen 3 offers a cost-effective solution for building AI-powered applications. Its capabilities in code generation, natural language understanding, and reasoning make it suitable for tasks ranging from chatbot development to data analysis.

Businesses

Enterprises can leverage Qwen 3 to enhance customer service through intelligent chatbots, automate content generation, and analyze vast datasets for insights. Its support for 119 languages ensures global applicability, catering to diverse markets.

Integration Tools

Qwen 3 supports integration with various tools and platforms:

- **SGLang and vLLM**: Facilitate efficient model serving and deployment. LinkedIn

- **Ollama**: Simplifies local deployment for development and testing.

- **MCP Compatibility**: Enables seamless integration with external databases, APIs, and tools, reducing engineering overhead. Milvus

These tools ensure that Qwen 3 can be integrated into existing workflows with minimal friction, enhancing productivity and innovation.

Qwen 3 stands as a powerful, open-source AI model that offers flexibility, scalability, and accessibility. Its availability across multiple platforms, permissive licensing, and integration capabilities make it a valuable asset for developers and businesses alike. By embracing Qwen 3, users can harness the potential of advanced AI to drive innovation and efficiency in their respective domains.

Chapter 6

Performance and Benchmarks

The Global Arena: Qwen 3 vs. GPT-4, Claude, Gemini, and LLaMA

In the ever-evolving field of artificial intelligence, the performance of a model is measured not only by the architecture it runs on but by how it fares against its global peers. Qwen 3 enters this arena competing with industry leaders like OpenAI's GPT-4, Anthropic's Claude, Google's Gemini, and

Meta's LLaMA. While each of these models has its own unique strengths, Qwen 3 is rapidly gaining attention for its strong performance across both general-purpose and specialized tasks.

GPT-4, widely considered the industry gold standard, excels at reasoning, summarization, and instruction-following. Claude is known for its alignment and safety-first approach, offering a chat experience that prioritizes human-like understanding and low hallucination rates. Gemini boasts multimodal capabilities at scale, integrating text, images, audio, and even video into a single system. Meanwhile, LLaMA targets efficiency and customization, becoming a favorite among researchers and smaller-scale deployments.

What sets Qwen 3 apart is its exceptional multilingual support, extended context window, and powerful hybrid architecture combining dense and sparse models. These features make it a formidable competitor, particularly in tasks that require long-form comprehension, diverse linguistic fluency, or hybrid reasoning.

Comparative Strengths and Weaknesses

Where Qwen 3 Leads

- **Multilingual Performance**: Qwen 3 supports 119 languages and dialects, significantly more than GPT-4 and Claude. This positions it as an ideal model for global deployment in non-

English-speaking regions.

- **Context Window**: With a 128,000-token context window, Qwen 3 enables deep comprehension of long-form documents. GPT-4 offers similar extended contexts in its GPT-4 Turbo version, but Qwen's open accessibility gives it an edge in certain academic and research domains.

- **Open-Source Accessibility**: Unlike GPT-4, Claude, and Gemini, which are closed-source, Qwen 3 is open-sourced under the Apache 2.0 license. This offers transparency and flexibility for researchers and developers.

- **Hybrid Architecture (MoE)**: Qwen 3 combines dense and sparse structures through Mixture-of-Experts, optimizing performance and efficiency. This feature is still experimental in most Western models.

Where It Lags

- **Instruction Tuning**: GPT-4 and Claude still lead in instruction following, zero-shot tasks, and nuanced dialog understanding. Qwen 3, while powerful, occasionally requires more prompt engineering.

- **Safety and Alignment**: Claude and Gemini shine in producing safe, non-biased, and aligned outputs. Qwen 3 is improving in this regard, but additional safety fine-tuning might be needed for sensitive applications.

- **Multimodality Integration**: While Qwen-VL extends capabilities beyond text, it is not yet as seamless as Gemini or GPT-4's multimodal versions.

Specific Tasks Where Qwen 3 Excels

Language Translation

Qwen 3 demonstrates high accuracy in multilingual translation, including low-resource languages. Its training on diverse tokens across 119 languages enables natural-sounding output and consistent grammar, often rivaling professional-grade translation tools.

Long-Form Document Analysis

Thanks to its 128K context window, Qwen 3 can handle legal documents, research papers, and entire books in a single pass. This allows for better summarization, citation mapping, and in-depth content parsing compared to models restricted to 32K or 8K tokens.

Code Reasoning and Generation

Qwen 3 performs particularly well in programming tasks, especially in languages like Python, C++, and JavaScript. Benchmarks like HumanEval and MBPP (Mostly Basic Programming Problems) show it achieving competitive, sometimes superior, results against GPT-4 and LLaMA.

Multilingual Summarization and Dialogue

Its extensive multilingual capabilities allow Qwen 3 to summarize content, generate news briefs, or hold conversations in native dialects. This is an advantage in regions with diverse language needs, like Southeast Asia, Africa, or the Middle East.

Hybrid Logical Reasoning

Qwen 3's hybrid MoE design allows it to selectively activate expert networks based on input complexity. This makes it more efficient in responding to logic-based queries without compromising computational resources.

Benchmarking Qwen 3: The Numbers That Matter

MMLU (Massive Multitask Language Understanding)

Qwen 3-72B achieves competitive scores on MMLU, a benchmark evaluating knowledge across 57 tasks. It nearly matches or even exceeds GPT-4 in multiple subjects such as STEM, humanities, and professional areas.

Big-Bench Hard (BBH)

On BBH, which focuses on advanced reasoning, Qwen 3-72B and Qwen 3-110B perform on par with Claude 2, particularly in tasks requiring deductive logic, analogical reasoning, and classification.

HumanEval and MBPP

Qwen 3 outperforms Claude 2 and LLaMA 2 in code generation benchmarks. It solves complex programming problems with fewer attempts and higher accuracy. The 72B and 110B models show a consistent upward trend in solving real-world coding challenges.

ARC (AI2 Reasoning Challenge)

Qwen 3 excels in the ARC benchmark, designed to test scientific reasoning in grade-school level questions. Its mixture-of-experts model appears to adapt better than purely dense models in these reasoning-intensive tasks.

GSM8K (Grade School Math)

In math word problems, Qwen 3's structured reasoning trails GPT-4 slightly but remains ahead of most open-source models. It's particularly efficient when using chain-of-thought prompting.

Community Feedback and Expert Opinions

Researchers and AI developers have lauded Qwen 3's open-sourced architecture, long context window, and language versatility. On forums such as GitHub and Hugging Face, users report that Qwen 3 performs reliably in summarization, translation, and creative writing.

Academic papers from institutions in China, Singapore, and Europe have begun citing Qwen 3 in comparative studies, indicating a growing trust in its performance. Experts highlight the model's efficient routing through MoE layers and its tokenizer's ability to reduce semantic loss in multilingual outputs.

Industry observers suggest that Qwen 3 may set a precedent for East-Asian models challenging the dominance of Western AI tools. Its high benchmark scores and open development pipeline mark a strategic shift towards decentralizing innovation in the global AI space.

Real-World Case Studies and Deployments

Education

In universities across China, Qwen 3 is being piloted to assist with grading, tutoring, and research assistance. Its high accuracy in

Chinese dialects makes it ideal for language learning tools.

Healthcare

Medical research teams are exploring Qwen 3 for summarizing research papers, translating medical texts, and generating patient interaction scripts. Its ability to comprehend long documents enhances efficiency in diagnostics support.

E-commerce

Alibaba has integrated early versions of Qwen into its customer service systems. Qwen 3 builds on that foundation with improved intent recognition and multilingual chat capabilities for global storefronts.

Media and Publishing

News agencies use Qwen 3 to summarize articles, generate headlines, and translate press releases in multiple languages. Its capacity to maintain tone and clarity across languages gives it a competitive edge.

Challenges and Future Outlook

Despite its strong performance, Qwen 3 still faces several challenges:

- **Fine-Tuning Needs**: It occasionally requires specific prompt templates to achieve optimal results.

- **Compute Costs**: Large MoE models demand significant resources to train and deploy at scale.

- **Data Curation**: Continued quality control over training data is crucial to avoid biased or outdated outputs.

- **Safety and Alignment**: Qwen 3 needs further development to match the alignment levels of Claude and Gemini.

However, its roadmap hints at further breakthroughs:

- Future versions may integrate even larger MoE layers.

- Expansion into audio, vision, and video inputs is expected.

- More collaborative research papers and multilingual benchmarks are underway.

Qwen 3 is not merely catching up with global AI giants—it is paving its own path. With its deep architecture, multilingual fluency, and open philosophy, Qwen 3 has earned a place among the best. As it continues to improve, it could redefine the benchmark for what open-source AI can truly achieve.

Chapter 7

Real-World Applications

Empowering Industries with Qwen 3

As Qwen 3 matures into one of the most powerful language models in the world, its utility across various sectors is becoming increasingly evident. Businesses, researchers, and creatives are actively integrating Qwen 3 into their workflows, transforming how tasks are performed and solutions are delivered. The real-world impact of Qwen 3 isn't just about its raw power—it's about accessibility, adaptability, and actual deployment.

Business Integration and Digital Transformation

Businesses are leveraging Qwen 3 to automate customer service, analyze large datasets, and generate high-quality content at scale. For instance, e-commerce platforms use Qwen 3 to power intelligent chatbots that handle customer queries with human-like comprehension. These bots are not only multilingual but also contextually aware, capable of remembering prior interactions to provide consistent and coherent support.

In financial services, Qwen 3 assists in regulatory compliance by parsing through vast amounts of legal documents to flag inconsistencies or risky behaviors. It also provides predictive insights by processing market data, aiding analysts in making data-driven decisions. Marketing teams are embracing Qwen 3 for campaign ideation, product descriptions, and real-time trend analysis, accelerating content delivery while maintaining high quality.

Academia and Research Advancement

In research, Qwen 3's multilingual capabilities are breaking down linguistic barriers that have long hindered global collaboration. Researchers use it to translate and summarize academic papers, propose hypotheses, and even assist in the design of experiments. Because Qwen 3 is open-source under the Apache 2.0 license, academic institutions can tailor the model to their specific needs without prohibitive costs.

Its ability to analyze complex language patterns and generate coherent explanations makes it a valuable tool for educators, enabling the development of AI tutors that personalize instruction based on each student's learning style and pace. Educational institutions are embedding Qwen 3 in digital learning platforms to make education more interactive and accessible, particularly in underserved regions.

Creative Industries: From Imagination to Execution

Creatives, too, are turning to Qwen 3 to augment their craft. Writers use it to brainstorm ideas, refine dialogue, and overcome writer's block. Filmmakers and game developers rely on it for generating plots, character arcs, and world-building descriptions. Qwen 3's multimodal capabilities extend its usefulness into art and design—helping artists convert textual prompts into detailed visual concepts.

One example includes using Qwen 3 to storyboard animations, where the AI generates sequential scene descriptions based on a script. Graphic designers leverage the model to write compelling copy that matches visual themes, enabling more cohesive creative productions.

Case Study: E-Commerce and Customer Experience

Alibaba, the developer behind Qwen 3, uses the model extensively in its own e-commerce ecosystem. On platforms like Taobao and Tmall, Qwen 3 enhances user experience by offering personalized product recommendations and instant query responses. It analyzes user behavior to predict preferences and tailors marketing content accordingly.

This integration has improved customer satisfaction and reduced cart abandonment rates, as users are met with accurate answers and relevant suggestions throughout their shopping journey. Moreover, sellers benefit from AI-generated product descriptions, titles, and campaign strategies—all driven by Qwen 3.

Translation and Cross-Cultural Communication

Qwen 3's support for 119 languages and dialects makes it ideal for translation tasks. In international business, this means contracts, emails, and marketing materials can be accurately and contextually translated. It's especially valuable for NGOs and governments working in multilingual environments, as it aids in bridging communication gaps that would otherwise require extensive human resources.

Language learning apps are also integrating Qwen 3 to create interactive lessons, quizzes, and conversational practice scenarios. The model's understanding of colloquialisms and cultural nuances ensures that translations aren't just literal but retain the intended meaning.

Developer Empowerment and Software Engineering

Qwen 3 is empowering developers by automating routine coding tasks and accelerating debugging processes. It assists in writing functions, generating documentation, and refactoring legacy code. For startups and independent developers, this means faster iteration and reduced development costs.

In enterprise environments, Qwen 3 supports DevOps pipelines by analyzing logs, predicting system failures, and recommending optimizations. It also facilitates onboarding by creating interactive technical documentation tailored to different skill levels, from novice to expert.

AI in Education: Personalization at Scale

Educational technology companies are embedding Qwen 3 into virtual tutors that assess student performance in real-time. By analyzing answers and response patterns, the AI adjusts the difficulty level and provides targeted feedback. This form of personalized learning has been shown to improve retention rates and student satisfaction.

Educators also use Qwen 3 to generate quizzes, assignments, and reading material that aligns with curriculum standards.

Language teachers employ it for grammar corrections, pronunciation feedback, and vocabulary enhancement exercises.

Content Generation and Media

Media organizations utilize Qwen 3 for generating news articles, headlines, and social media posts. Its ability to maintain a consistent tone and style makes it ideal for producing branded content. Editors rely on the model to draft summaries, captions, and scripts—significantly reducing production time.

Podcast producers and YouTubers use Qwen 3 to brainstorm episode outlines, generate titles with high click-through potential, and draft dialogue. This integration of AI into content creation not only boosts productivity but also fuels innovation by enabling creators to explore new formats and topics with minimal effort.

Future Outlook: Scaling Real-World Impact

As Qwen 3 continues to evolve, its real-world applications will become even more nuanced and impactful. With advancements in multimodal understanding and larger context windows, the model will support increasingly sophisticated workflows across sectors. Future use cases may include real-time financial forecasting, fully autonomous customer support agents, and AI-powered legal assistants.

Businesses and institutions that invest early in understanding and deploying Qwen 3 are positioning themselves at the forefront of the AI revolution. As the technology matures and the ecosystem around it grows, Qwen 3 will likely become a foundational tool—akin to the role played by electricity or the internet in past industrial shifts.

Chapter 8

Ethical, Strategic, and Global Implications

China's AI Strategy and Geopolitical Vision

Qwen 3 is not merely a technological achievement—it is a strategic asset that aligns with China's long-term goals in the global AI arms race. As nations compete to dominate artificial intelligence, Qwen 3 serves as a symbol of China's ambition to lead not only in AI research but also in the deployment of trustworthy, high-performing models.

Beijing has outlined national strategies to make China the world leader in AI by 2030, and Alibaba's open-source initiatives like Qwen 3 are a core component of this vision. By releasing such a powerful model into the global ecosystem, China demonstrates its technological prowess while also projecting influence through open collaboration.

Transparency, Safety, and AI Ethics

One of the most crucial topics in modern AI is transparency. Alibaba's decision to open-source Qwen 3 under the permissive Apache 2.0 license signals a commitment to transparency. It allows developers and researchers worldwide to audit, fine-tune, and build upon the model.

That said, transparency alone does not guarantee ethical usage. To mitigate risks of misuse, Alibaba has implemented safety guardrails and content moderation features directly into Qwen 3's architecture. These include filters that prevent the generation of harmful, biased, or misleading outputs, as well as sandbox environments for safe experimentation.

This approach strikes a balance between innovation and responsibility—ensuring that the model can be both powerful and safe. While questions remain about long-term governance, Alibaba's early efforts at AI alignment and control are in line with global best practices.

Open-Source Freedom vs. Control

Open-sourcing a model like Qwen 3 is a double-edged sword. On one hand, it democratizes access to cutting-edge AI, enabling innovation at a global scale. Startups, academic institutions, and independent developers gain access to tools that were once the exclusive domain of tech giants.

On the other hand, it raises concerns about control and misuse. Open-source models can be repurposed for malicious tasks—from generating deepfakes to automating cyberattacks. This dilemma is at the heart of the debate between freedom and control in AI development.

Alibaba's solution involves coupling open-source distribution with robust usage guidelines and default safety configurations. This strategy encourages responsible use while still fostering a culture of open innovation. It sets a precedent for how powerful AI tools can be shared without compromising security.

Implications for Global AI Competition

The release of Qwen 3 intensifies the competition between global AI superpowers. While U.S.-based models like GPT-4, Claude, and Gemini dominate English-speaking markets, Qwen 3 offers an alternative rooted in linguistic and cultural diversity. Its support for 119 languages is not just a technical feat—it's a geopolitical strategy to engage non-Western audiences.

In regions where Western tech companies face regulatory or political barriers, Qwen 3 provides a compelling alternative. Governments, enterprises, and developers may prefer a model that is not tethered to U.S. policies or infrastructure. This enhances China's soft power and opens new avenues for digital diplomacy.

Moreover, the sheer scale and performance of Qwen 3 push the industry forward. Competing firms are now under pressure to innovate faster, adopt open standards, and reconsider their own transparency policies. In this way, Qwen 3 not only redefines what AI can do—it reshapes how AI is built, governed, and shared across borders.

The Stakes of an Open AI Future

The ethical, strategic, and global implications of Qwen 3 are profound. As one of the most capable and accessible models on the planet, it has the potential to uplift communities, transform industries, and influence the trajectory of international AI development.

Its openness challenges the status quo and invites a more inclusive future—one where technological power is not hoarded but distributed. Yet with that openness comes a responsibility to manage risk, maintain safety, and uphold shared values.

Qwen 3 is not just a tool—it is a turning point. How we choose to use, regulate, and evolve such models will define not only the next generation of AI but the shape of our global society for decades to come.

Chapter 9

The Future of Qwen and AI in China

The rapidly advancing field of artificial intelligence has fundamentally altered the landscape of technology worldwide. In the case of Qwen 3, Alibaba's AI model, the future holds even greater promise, with a trajectory that could redefine what is possible with large language models (LLMs). As Qwen 3 continues to evolve, a close examination of what may lie ahead for its successors, the ripple effects on global tech players, and the broader impact on the perception of Chinese AI offers a fascinating glimpse into the future of AI development.

What Might Qwen 4 Look Like?

The Roadmap for Improvement

Qwen 4 is not merely a speculative extension of its predecessor but a potential leap toward more sophisticated AI capabilities that address both the limitations and opportunities presented by the current technological landscape. To understand what Qwen 4 might look like, it is crucial to look at the limitations and the advancements made in the preceding versions, as well as the key areas that need attention in future iterations.

Qwen 3 has already established itself with a strong foundation in natural language understanding, reasoning, multilingual fluency, and multimodal capabilities. However, like any cutting-edge technology, Qwen 3 is not without its challenges. The primary areas for improvement include:

1. **Scaling with Efficiency**: While Qwen 3 boasts impressive performance, particularly with its hybrid dense and sparse models, scalability remains a core challenge. Future iterations, such as Qwen 4, are likely to adopt even more efficient hybrid models or further optimize Mixture-of-Experts (MoE) systems to enable broader applicability without incurring excessive computational costs. This could potentially allow Qwen 4 to handle even larger datasets

while maintaining a reasonable balance between performance and energy efficiency.

2. **Multimodal Integration**: Qwen 3 has already demonstrated remarkable capabilities in processing both text and image data. However, a full-fledged multimodal system—one that can seamlessly integrate and reason across a wider variety of inputs, including sound, video, and other sensory data—could be a key feature of Qwen 4. This would enable more natural, human-like interactions in various real-world applications, from advanced robotics to immersive virtual environments.

3. **Ethical and Bias Mitigation**: One area where Qwen 4 could potentially lead is in the improvement of ethical AI development and bias mitigation. Given the increasing awareness of AI's societal impact, future versions will likely emphasize better detection, correction, and prevention of biases in model outputs. Additionally, transparency regarding decision-making processes and ensuring the accountability of AI systems could become integral features of Qwen 4.

4. **Higher-level Reasoning and Creativity**: Although Qwen 3 excels at generating relevant and contextually accurate information, Qwen 4 could take this further by

enhancing the model's ability to engage in complex, multi-step reasoning and creative problem-solving. This could be particularly useful in domains such as scientific research, creative writing, and strategic decision-making.

5. **Adaptation and Customization**: Personalized AI that adapts to the user's specific needs and preferences could be another breakthrough. Qwen 4 may enable more dynamic and customizable interaction, with features that allow the model to fine-tune itself based on the type of user it's engaging with, whether they are a researcher, a creative professional, or

a business executive.

The Role of Quantum Computing

As quantum computing continues to progress, there is a possibility that future versions of Qwen may leverage quantum algorithms for processing and analyzing data at an unprecedented speed. Quantum computing holds the potential to revolutionize AI by enabling exponential improvements in performance, especially in complex tasks such as real-time data analysis, large-scale optimizations, and machine learning model training. Although this may not be immediately realized in Qwen 4, it's a development worth anticipating.

How This Model Might Influence Other Tech Players

Qwen 3, and potentially its successor Qwen 4, is poised to reshape the competitive landscape of global AI. The influence of Alibaba's model extends beyond its technical capabilities and into strategic and competitive realms. Several key outcomes can be expected as Qwen 3's impact spreads.

Pushing the Boundaries of AI Development

As one of the most advanced AI models developed in China, Qwen is helping to elevate the country's position in the global AI race. The rapid advancement of Qwen models puts considerable pressure on tech giants such as OpenAI, Google, and Meta, challenging them to push the boundaries of what their own systems can do. While many of these companies have made significant strides with models like GPT, BERT, and LaMDA, Qwen's hybrid architecture, its focus on multilingualism, and its advanced reasoning abilities may prompt other companies to refine their own models in order to stay competitive.

For instance, the integration of the Mixture-of-Experts (MoE) system could push competitors to explore similar techniques or adopt entirely new architectures that improve computational efficiency while maintaining performance. Additionally, Qwen's approach to transparency in AI development may inspire other firms to adopt more open-source methodologies, making their AI systems more accessible to a wider range of developers and innovators.

Strengthening China's Tech Diplomacy

Qwen 3, and the AI industry in general, have become a cornerstone of China's tech diplomacy. The model is not only a technical asset but a geopolitical one. As China strives to become a leader in the global AI race, the successful development and deployment of Qwen 3 helps position the country as an AI powerhouse. This puts China in direct competition with the United States and other leading nations in AI development, creating both opportunities and challenges.

By creating highly capable AI models like Qwen 3, Alibaba and other Chinese tech giants are influencing global standards and policy discussions related to AI ethics, safety, and regulations. As such, the model could play a pivotal role in shaping the future trajectory of AI governance, especially as governments around the world begin to develop regulatory frameworks for advanced AI systems.

The Role of Qwen in Reshaping Global Perception of Chinese AI

For years, Chinese AI has faced skepticism and, at times, suspicion from the global community. Historically, many have viewed Chinese AI development with caution, often associating it with concerns about data privacy, authoritarian control, and the potential for misuse. However, Qwen 3 is proving that China is capable of producing high-quality, sophisticated AI models that can compete on the global stage.

From Controversy to Credibility

Qwen 3 is helping to shift the global perception of Chinese AI from one of suspicion to one of credibility. The transparency in the development and release of the model, the commitment to open-sourcing it under the Apache 2.0 license, and its demonstrated abilities in a variety of applications all contribute to a more positive view of Chinese AI.

Furthermore, by offering the model to the international community and encouraging collaboration, Alibaba has taken steps to ensure that Qwen is seen not just as a tool for Chinese interests, but as a global asset. This could lead to greater cross-border partnerships and cooperation in AI research and development, fostering an environment of shared innovation.

Overcoming Challenges

While the success of Qwen 3 may mark a turning point, China's AI industry still faces challenges in terms of international acceptance. Concerns regarding ethical implications, data sovereignty, and the regulatory environment persist. However, the proactive approach taken by Alibaba in ensuring the model is both ethical and safe, alongside its transparency efforts, may help alleviate some of these concerns.

As Qwen 4 and future iterations continue to emerge, the role of Chinese AI will likely shift from a reactive, defensive stance to a more proactive, leading one. With advancements in AI governance and ethical frameworks, Chinese AI models like Qwen could serve as examples of how to balance innovation with responsibility.

Final Reflections on Responsible AI Development

The rapid pace of AI development necessitates that responsible AI practices be at the forefront of every new iteration. As we look ahead to Qwen 4 and the broader future of AI, it is important to reflect on the ethical responsibilities that come with creating such powerful technologies.

AI models like Qwen have the potential to change society in profound ways. They can improve healthcare, revolutionize education, enhance creativity, and provide solutions to complex global problems. However, with such power comes the need for careful consideration of the societal, cultural, and ethical implications.

In the future, AI development must prioritize transparency, accountability, fairness, and inclusivity. Models like Qwen 4 will be successful not just because they perform well, but because they are developed and used responsibly. Ensuring that AI benefits all of humanity requires ongoing collaboration between tech companies, governments, ethicists, and the public to establish global norms and standards.

China's approach to AI development, exemplified by Qwen, is a crucial part of this global conversation. By setting an example in both innovation and responsibility, China can play a key role in shaping a future where AI contributes positively to society on a global scale.

This conclusion wraps up the discussion on Qwen's future by highlighting the key areas where improvements are anticipated, how the model's success impacts other tech companies, and how China's AI landscape is evolving to change the global perception. It emphasizes the importance of responsible AI development as a critical aspect of the future of AI technologies.

Conclusion

As we conclude our exploration of Qwen 3 and its future, we have traversed a comprehensive journey through the capabilities, applications, and implications of this advanced AI model. From understanding its robust natural language processing abilities to examining its impact on global competition, the role of Qwen in shaping the AI landscape has been nothing short of transformative.

Recap of What Readers Have Learned

Throughout this guide, readers have gained a thorough understanding of Qwen 3's core strengths, its architectural design, and the technological advancements that make it a significant player in the AI field. We've explored:

- **Qwen's Technical Foundations**: From its multilingual capabilities and multimodal abilities to its advanced reasoning and code generation features, Qwen 3 demonstrates the future of AI with its highly versatile models.

- **Practical Applications**: We have seen real-world examples of how businesses, researchers, and creatives are leveraging Qwen 3 to revolutionize industries, from customer support and software development to content generation and education.

- **Performance Benchmarks**: A deep dive into the comparison between Qwen 3 and other leading AI models, including GPT-4, Claude, and Gemini, has highlighted both its strengths and areas for improvement, making it clear where Qwen shines and where it might lag behind.

- **Ethical and Geopolitical Implications**: We've explored the ethical considerations around AI transparency and the role of Chinese tech companies like Alibaba in reshaping global perceptions of AI, with a particular focus on Qwen's evolving place within the broader geopolitical landscape.

- **The Future of Qwen**: Finally, we examined what the next iterations of Qwen might look like and how advancements in AI will influence the competitive dynamics within the global tech market.

Encouragement for Further Exploration, Testing, and Building

The world of AI is evolving at an astonishing pace, and Qwen 3 represents just one part of a broader, rapidly advancing ecosystem. As we've seen, Qwen is already a powerful tool for numerous industries, but its future potential is far from fully realized. For those in the field of AI development, this is a pivotal moment.

We encourage you to continue exploring the capabilities of Qwen 3 and future models. Whether you're an AI developer, a business professional, or an academic researcher, hands-on experience is invaluable. Testing the limits of these models in real-world scenarios will allow you to uncover new possibilities, refine existing applications, and perhaps even unlock innovative solutions that haven't yet been imagined.

The open-source nature of Qwen 3 offers a unique opportunity for experimentation. Developers, especially those interested in advancing the AI field, should take full advantage of the model's open licensing to build new features, tweak the architecture, or adapt the model to specific use cases. The more we engage with these tools, the more we contribute to shaping the future of AI technology.

A Note on How to Stay Updated on Qwen's Evolution

AI is a rapidly changing field, and staying updated on the latest developments in Qwen and similar models is critical to remaining at the forefront of this technological revolution. To ensure you are always informed about Qwen's evolution, here are some strategies:

1. **Follow Qwen on Key Platforms**: Stay connected with the Qwen community on platforms like GitHub, Hugging Face, and ModelScope. These platforms are where developers and researchers share updates, discuss new findings, and release model

improvements. Keep an eye out for new releases and updates to Qwen, as they often come with added features, bug fixes, and performance enhancements.

2. **Engage with Online Communities**: Communities on platforms like Reddit, Stack Overflow, and AI-specific forums are invaluable for discussions, troubleshooting, and staying informed about real-world use cases and breakthroughs. Being part of such communities can also provide insight into the latest AI research and practical applications.

3. **Subscribe to AI News Sources**: There are numerous tech publications

and blogs dedicated to AI advancements. Resources like TechCrunch, Wired, and VentureBeat regularly cover major updates in AI and offer expert opinions on trends and innovations. Subscribing to newsletters from AI-focused companies like OpenAI, Google Research, and Alibaba's AI division will ensure that you don't miss any important announcements or developments.

4. **Attend Conferences and Webinars**: AI and machine learning conferences, such as NeurIPS, ICML, and CVPR, are perfect opportunities to stay ahead of the curve. Many companies, including Alibaba, often

unveil their latest technologies and models at these events. Webinars and online events also provide access to discussions with experts on the cutting edge of AI.

5. **Experiment with New Releases**: As Qwen 3 evolves, new versions will continue to be released, potentially with expanded capabilities, optimizations, and even completely new features. By regularly testing the newest versions of Qwen models, you will be at the forefront of innovation and gain firsthand experience with how the AI landscape is shifting.

By staying engaged with these resources and continuing to explore the vast potential of Qwen and other AI models, you can contribute to shaping the future of AI. This field is still in its infancy, and those who dive deep, experiment, and collaborate will be the ones to drive the next wave of technological innovation.

Thank you for embarking on this journey through Qwen's present and future. The world of AI is only beginning to unfold its full potential, and with tools like Qwen, we are all part of a transformative movement that will impact nearly every aspect of life in the years to come.